How To Write Better:

Take Your Writing To The Next Level Creating Texts That Readers Want To Read

Legal & Disclaimer

whether directly or indirectly, of any advice or information presented, whether for breach of contract, tort, negligence, personal injury, criminal intent, or under any other cause of action. You agree to accept all risks of using the information presented in this book.

You agree that by continuing to read this book, where appropriate and/or necessary, you shall consult a professional (including but not limited to your doctor, attorney, or financial advisor or such other advisor as needed) before using any of the suggested remedies, techniques, or information in this book.

Table of Contents

1. Introduction

Once a person has learned the art of basic writing they should work to take their skills to the next level to start generating some income out of their skill. There are many writers in the world who are creating quality content and in return are making money from it. Be it running a tech blog, a health care website, an educational page that serves students, if you have the knack of generating the quality content, you should be contributing in the field.

Before you start confusing yourself with the term quality content, let's have it explained. Understanding the basic rules of writing and creating a good piece of work all can fall under the term quality content. There are some basic rules and points that each one of you should keep in mind while writing any piece. This is especially necessary if you want to have your work ranked at a better position on the search engines.

"Good" content and "Quality" content are two different terms that carry different meanings. In the beginning, search engines' had a really simple algorithm to rank the content. All they needed was the existence of the content, the keyword inclusion and the number of times it was included and repeated in the content. Later on, with a major upgrade, the criteria was rearranged. Now the search engines look through the content and rank it on the basis of the quality of content that it may have. Not only the search engines, but a reader also wants to read the content with some quality. No one wants to waste their time reading a content or book which is not up to the mark.

There are some top components which every writer should keep in mind while creating a content.

1.1. Is it informational?

When the content of a book is of high quality, it doesn't just skim over the issues, it discusses it in detail and provides answers and information about it. There should be a new and unique detail about it instead of only repeating what many others also wrote previously. Adding some more information to the already existing issue will make your content stand out among others.

1.2. Entertaining & Catchy

The best content available now is the one which is to the point and shows passion to the readers. This makes people want to get engaged with the content. However, there are technical and emotional factors involved with this too.

The technical factors involve the content types for example videos, quizzes and list articles. They tend to perform really well as compared to other sort of content.

The emotional factors include things like utility, emotional value and shock-value.

1.3. Uniqueness

Anyone can rewrite an article after performing a little google research but that will never earn you the best place among other writers and content. Keeping this is mind, add something to the content which gives it a new favor and makes it your unique work.

1.4. Is it Adding Value?

If your content is just another version of already existing 5000+ pages on the web, you are not contributing to the knowledge of the readers in any way. Similarly, if the sleeping princess will be woken up by the kiss of the prince, *again*, then it is better she keeps sleeping.

1.5. Have You Added Your Personal Voice?

It is very essential that your article or story has your personal voice in it. Personalized material get to read more as the readers associate it with the writer. It also adds fun to your writing and makes it different among the rest. So don't hesitate adding your own flavor in the writing.

1.6. Optimize Your Content

This is especially important if you are aiming to rank your content on the web. For example if your run your own blog, you need to make sure that you have optimized your content efficiently. Search Engine Optimization (SEO) is an entirely separate topic on its own but there are few things about it that you should keep in mind. They include, target keywords, high quality images, engaging headings, optimizing page loading time, and many other elements.

It is very easy to create content when your focus is your reader. Only by adopting this approach you will be able to deliver a very high quality content for your audience. Whenever you start writing, ask yourself the following questions, they will help you find the right approach for your new writing project.

- Who is my target audience?
- What issues do they have?
- Will they find the information relevant that I am providing?
- Which is the popular content in my niche?
- Am I adding anything unique or original which will be benefiting my readers?

Once you get all the answers to these questions you can consider yourself ready to start working on the project.

2. Principles of Good Writing

As the means of communication advanced, the methods of writing evolved as well. Most of the people started using shortcuts in writing and this has led to an overall decline in the quality of writing, in this author's opinion. Learning good writing skills is just as hard as learning a new language. Using correct grammar and punctuation, applying appropriate words for appropriate events, using clear language in order to avoid misunderstanding and miscommunication are all important. While speaking it is easier for the listener to understand what we actually intend to say, however, it gets a little harder in the written form if the sentences are not able to convey the right meaning.

If you follow the principles of good writing, it will help you to enhance your art and you will be able to deliver high quality material very soon. Keep working on each one of these tips and follow them up in your writings after finishing each draft as well.

2.1. Correct Use of Grammar

Grammatical errors are not forgivable in any case. Grammar is basically the structure of a writing and not being able to build the structure accurately will never give you a sound foundation. If the basic structure of your writing has gone wrong then it doesn't matter how strong message you were trying to give to your readers. No one will be interested in finding the hidden message in your incorrectly written piece.

2.2. Active Voice

Make sure you are using active voice in all your writings. Active voice is easy to remember and understand. A very easy an old example about this is "the cat ate the mouse" and "the mouse was eaten by the cat". While the subject here is cat so it should always be in the beginning of the sentence. Usage of passive sentences can confuse the reader and he can forget what you were actually talking about. Using active voice can also reduce the length of your sentences, which is another good practice in writing.

2.3. Brief Sentences

Nothing bores a reader more than getting to read really lengthy sentences. They are indeed the communication killers. It is very essential to keep your sentences as short as possible. Along with keeping the sentences short, you also need to keep them simple. Using simple words in your writings is also very important as a single writer has millions of readers from different backgrounds. If you are using difficult words for which a user needs to open their dictionary again and again, you are losing a reader.

Difficult words doesn't make you sound like a genius but it makes it difficult for your reader to go through your writings without using a dictionary. When you're writing, you should keep in mind that your audience will be varying so use the words which will be easily understandable by everyone.

2.4. Sentence Structure

The sentence structure in your writing needs to support your voice. Keep a very clear beginning, middle and an end. Your sentence structure also tells where you are leading to further in your writing. Twisting the sentence structure and making it grim in an attempt to turn it into something interesting, will be making it difficult for the reader to understand what you are trying to convey. As mentioned earlier, it becomes much more difficult to understand the thoughts when a person is reading it, since the writer is not there to make them understand their point. So it is the writer's duty to keep their readers on track.

2.5. Correct Choice of Words

Having a good vocabulary is very important for a writer. However, knowing when and how to use it is equally important too. Words that you use will determine your style as well. Make your writings go easy on the reader and use the words which will convey positive, negative, weak or strong message as per your writing demand.

2.6. Keep Your Audience in Mind

Unless you are writing personal journal, keeping your audience in mind is very important. Your writing style should differ according to the target audience. For example, 5 year olds cannot read the same content which is for a grown science scholar. You style should differ in every writing so that you can entertain different audience accordingly.

2.7. Punctuation

Just like grammar mistakes cannot be neglected, punctuation mistakes cannot taken lightly. Commas are ignored while typing text messages but they cannot be ignored when you are writing a formal letter or a meaningful piece of writing. The lack of punctuation can make a sentence sound really bizarre. For example, "Let's eat, baby" and "Let's eat baby" have a huge difference between them which is made only by use of a simple comma.

2.8. Proofread

Take multiple shots while performing proofreading. Your writing will be made perfect by repeatedly proofreading it. Re-read the content at least 3 to 4 times before marking it as final. You will be able to mark several grammar and punctuation mistakes at the end of every proofreading exercise. Repeat this until you are completely satisfied with your work.

3. Basics of Good Writing

Principles and basics of a good writing are nearly same, however, this is added here again to summarize all the small important points which you need to keep in mind while writing your new piece.

- [ ] A writing is considered good if it has a clear purpose.
- [ ] The reader can extract the point which you are trying to convey.
- [ ] You have added enough supporting information in support of your point.
- [ ] The information you have added should always revolve around the main topic. You can add some extra bits of relevant information but make sure that the added information also stay around the main topic and don't divert the reader elsewhere.
- [ ] The words and sentences you have used should have a connection with the topic.
- [ ] Sentences should be concise, emphatic, and correct in every way.
- [ ] Use your own voice while writing, extract ideas if you need to but then add your own voice in the context so that the reader can associate it with you.

You cannot become a good writer in your first attempt. It will take a lot of time and practice to master the art of writing well. This is indeed good to know that the not all writers are born writers but many of them have learned and practiced to become one of the great writers. If someone is genuinely interested to enhance his/her skills, they can actually improve by working on it. Even the most famous and successful and renowned writers say that it is not easy to write sometimes. Always remember that discouraging yourself because you were not able to perform well the first time is never going to help.

Keep in mind that you are going to get better with time and practice. Two things which are always going to get you through anything is your consistency and determination. When you will start sharpening your skills, you will gain confidence and enjoy writing. If you find it difficult to write on any given topic today, then after developing your skill, not only will you start enjoying the process, you will also be able to write on any given topic.

Isaac Bashevis was once quoted by Valerie Wells in "Isaac B. Singer on Writing, Life, Love and Death" on August 4, 1991 and said:

"One is never happy. If a writer is too happy with his writing, something is wrong with him. A real writer always feels as if he hasn't done enough. This is the reason he has the ambition to rewrite, to publish things, and so on. The bad writers are very happy with what they do. They always seem surprised about how good they are. I would say that a real writer sees that he missed a lot of opportunities"

There is always room for improvement and it can be found by reading and re-reading what you already wrote. However, you need not to degrade yourself but see where and how you can improve your work. With constant practice and effort, you will be able to achieve the rank among good writers.

4. Successful Templates for Structuring Writing

The transition from a topic to outline to draft is really hard. There is absolutely no doubt about that. It might sound easy that all you need to do is to open a new document and start writing your article but it is never as easy as it may sound. A good writing always needs some work done before and some planning that how that article or story will progress. With a roughly planned document or outline beforehand, it becomes easy for you to move along with the flow when you start using it.

A best way to create a template is to note down all those points which you follow frequently in your writings. Then write the headings for all those points on which you will be working in detail. For example,

- A title
- Intro
- Body
  - Section I
  - Section II
  - Section III
- Conclusion & Closing

These are actually the basic components of any writing. We can modify it further according to our needs but the general outlook stays this way.

You can list down as many things as you want in the template which you will be following. However, make sure that your template covers all those points which you will require while completing your piece.

You can also choose to note down all the points in the numbered or bulleted form. But keep them in order, so that your reader won't feel distracted while reading it. Your article needs to have a logical sequence. This is known as the List Method of structuring.

Another very effective and useful way of structuring your writing is called Inverted Pyramid structuring. This was used by writers many years ago to deliver their stories via telegraph. The main idea of the writing is presented in the first paragraph of the writing mostly. This is an old method but it still has its value for news-style articles which need to present the main information upfront.

5. Bring out the best in you

Becoming a good writer is not something that happens overnight. It's a long process and takes a lot of time and practice to achieve the goal. Remember to not be hard on yourself if you think you are not doing well. A good writer is never satisfied with their work anyways.

If you are already writing, try to narrow down your niche, this will help broaden your audience. Keep in mind that jack of all trades is master of none. Focus on one thing so that you can put your best efforts in it. Make it your daily habit to write every day, even if it is just one paragraph. But that one paragraph should be well structured and planned. If you are fulfilling all the basic needs and practices of a writer, you will soon become a good writer and will be acknowledged by a huge number of fans as well.

Let's focus on the main parts of a writing and discuss the tips and tricks in detail:

5.1. Figure Out an Interesting and Catchy Topic

Readers will be drawn to your article by reading its title. If you have a plain, monotonous title then people will not be attracted to it like they should have been. Take the topic as the first look and first appearance of a person, if you don't find them attractive enough, there are very low chances that you will be drawn towards them. The same principle applies to articles and books as well. If you don't have a catchy title and an interesting topic then forget about getting a large volume of traffic or readers.

People now a days look for things that are different and entertaining. It's an art to be different, entertaining and then providing accurate details as well. Try to be that artist who can carve out a creative catchy title for their work.

5.2. Draw a Guideline for the Topic

Once you have chosen a topic and a niche, it is time for you to brainstorm and jot down all those points about which you can talk about in the body of your writing. Write as per your convenience. It can be long extensive paragraphs or bullet points. You can create the guideline as per your convenience.

5.3. Carry Out Extensive Research on the Topic

Once you are done making a sketch of the topic, you can now start researching. A single topic may comprise of several small topics or subtopics which can be researched and included in your content. Each subtopic can either become an exclusive chapter or follow the main heading in many subheadings.
While researching, make sure you write in accordance with the topic. If you added some extra information, try to bounce back to your main topic while keeping the writing in constant flow.

5.4. Create Catchy Subheadings

There can be several subheadings under a single topic and those subheadings might attract different readers. If you are writing about parenting, there will be parents who want to read about the reasons toddlers put everything in mouth, some would want to know why their babies face gastric issue often and there will be some who wants to know about the symptoms that their kids might have worm in their stomach. Now you have three different readers who want to know about three different things.

In such cases, it is recommended to use very catchy subheadings which can catch attention of the reader instantly and they can find their required information. This way many people will find relevant information in minimum time and don't have to scroll through pages looking for it.

5.5. Write Your Rough Draft and Wait a Day before Proofreading & Editing It

Give your mind a day's rest before you start proofreading your draft. This break will get the content out of your mind and when you will read it again, you will have a new perspective about it. This helps a lot while making changes and proofreading the document.

While proofreading you will notice repetition of words and some irrelevant information, without which the document will still sound complete. Struck of such words or sentences, even paragraphs if needed. If you have quality information in your writing, you do not need to increase the length of the document.

5.6. Have Other People Proofread & Edit Your Work

This really helps as you get to know what a reader thinks about your writings. Once you have proofread and edited the document, give it to a friend or a colleague who can read and further proofread it for you. You will get a further refined writing in the end.

After getting the proofread document from your ally, go through it again to see if the changes they have suggested are in accordance with what you were discussing in your writing or not. If they match your idea, keep them otherwise you can use your own proofreading as well.

6. Secrets to creating powerful introductions that grab readers' attention

Introductions make the first impression on your reader, and first impressions cannot be made twice. Writing a perfect intro and conclusion is considered the most difficult task in the writing, as they have a lot of responsibility on them. The introduction of your writing should be focused on grabbing the attention of the reader. It should be as interesting as possible and precise as well. Introduction should also give some background of your topic and talk about the relevant details.

A strong introduction will take your reader to the place where you want them to be. Your intro will be varying according to the niche you are writing on. Your readers will determine your argument, your writing style and the overall quality of the content you have added in your writing just by going through the introduction.

Here are some techniques that you may use to start your introduction. Remember that the techniques vary from the kind of your work. Fiction and scientific paper cannot have the same technique applied to write the introduction.

- ☐ Start your introduction with an intriguing example which relates to your topic. It will catch the reader's attention and they will want to know more about it.
- ☐ Use a provoking quotation which can be closely related to your argument. This will not work well for an academic paper, but, is very effective to be used for writing fiction or nonfiction.
- ☐ Create a puzzling scenario to gain readers curiosity.
- ☐ Write a vivid and unexpected sketch which compels the reader to continue reading.

☐ Include a thought provoking question in the beginning which can make the reader go on further with the writing, to find a satisfactory answer.

You should give special attention to the first sentence. It should be something useful, interesting and polished to intrigue reader's interest.

7. Secrets to creating writing that readers want to read

One thing that you should be emphasising on while writing is the quality of your work. A single page writing which has quality work on it can get you more readers than a 10 page writing which has less information and more junk information. There are also some minor mistakes that you should avoid to make your writing attractive to your readers.

Another very important tip to make improvements in your writings is to read more. The more you read, more it will help you to broaden your writing skills. As a musician cannot bring advancements in his/her work by not listening to music, similarly a writer cannot enhance his/her work if they don't invest their time reading. By reading other writer's work, not only you will be able to make an analysis about others but also learn that as a reader what compels and doesn't compels while reading any writing.

Here are some points that you should keep in mind if you are passionate about creating a huge fan following of your readers.

- ☐ Spend time writing and then assess it yourself. No one is perfect when they start writing but with constant effort and adequate time you can master the art of writing.
- ☐ Read a lot. Reading helps more than you can imagine. Find the right book for you and keep reading it.
- ☐ Associate your writings with the real world. Get real experiences and then interpret them in your writings wherever you can. Reader enjoys reading those things which can be associated with a writer.
- ☐ Make it a habit to write every day. It can be your journal or a small article on how things are happening in the world, but give this time every single day and write.

- Be expressive in your writings. It could be something that moves you emotionally, or make you cry. When a writer expresses their feelings in their writings, their readers can also feel the same emotions when they read it.

- If you think you cannot become a good writer since you do not have formal education in the subject, think again! A good writer doesn't need to shape their imagination according to school books. You should follow the basic writing rules, but cannot rely on the formal education to call yourself a good writer.

<u>8. Secrets to Create Powerful Endings</u>

It is human nature to get a nice closure to everything. When a reader has gone through all of your books but he finds a very vague and uninteresting closing in the end, he will get frustrated and this can make you lose a reader. Just like introduction, work hard on your ending as well. A powerful ending can give a reader the closure they deserve.

You should keep in mind while writing your ending is that it should be summarizing all the content of your writing. A reader who has spent his/her time reading your work deserves to get a justified end. If you have raised some questions in the whole content, make sure you answer them within the content or at least in the end. Don't leave the reader hanging and wondering about the answers of those questions.

Keep your ending logical and with the flow of the whole context. Do not add an abrupt ending at any cost. Abrupt endings are amusement killers, they should be avoided just the way you will avoid plague, or they will drive your readers away.

If you bake a cake you would know that taking it out of the oven earlier or keeping it in the oven for too long can ruin the cake. Writing is just like that. Elongate it more than required or end it all of a sudden without adding necessary details, will make it least interesting for the reader and ruin it.

9. <u>Most important writing pitfalls to avoid</u>

While writing specially the first draft for any document we make a lot of mistakes grammatically or in structure of sentence. We'll be discussing few important pitfalls you should avoid:

Directions

At all times read the directions carefully! If you do not understand the directions, make your research on that genre to clarify your doubts.

Excessive summarizing/lack of analysis

Your mission is to move past mere summary to help a reader understand your topic and analysis of the topic.

Plagiarism

Plagiarism is the usage of somebody else's effort, words, or thoughts, in any form, without appropriate credit. Whether you are mentioning, summarizing, or rephrasing in your own words, you must cite your sources.

Proofread

Proofread! Then let a third person proofread as well. More and more people proofread and more and more mistakes are discovered.

Tenses and Sentence Structure

Pay attention to shift verb tense only when essential. Frequent change in tenses or sentence formation gives a poor impact to the reader.

Passive voice

Use active voice as frequently as possible. Active voice usually is more brief and energetic than passive voice.

Title

If you want credit for your writing, then put your name on it along with a suitable title for your writing to make its own name in field of literature.

Writing Style

The style you should use be according to your reader. How do they think? Do they need long detailed explanations? Or do they prefer brief descriptions? So just pay attention!

10. Most important principles when writing

Process of Writing begins before we even jot down words to a piece of paper. It includes methods like critical thinking, communication, and creativity. Keeping in mind these methods following are some basic principles for general writing:

Prior to writing choose what the exact purpose of the writing is. Your every sentence should contribute in achieving purpose of whole writing.

- ☐ Have an idea about the reader of your writing and his/her capability to understand.
- ☐ While writing use simple and familiar words. Moreover, use a thesaurus side by side.
- ☐ At the opening and end of every topic check your writing according to this principle: first
- ☐ Introduce your readers to the topic.
- ☐ Explain the details of topic
- ☐ Conclude them with what you explained about.
- ☐ Make your writing understandable and avoid using meaningless long sentences.
- ☐ At the end of completing your first draft, read it thoroughly with your reader's point of view.
- ☐ As soon as you're confident about your writing, take a help from a third person to proofread your work before submitting the final draft.

These seven points are to be considered the basis of a general piece of writing. In the field of English literature we have a variety of writings worked upon e.g. Fiction, Non-Fiction, Novel, Drama, Fantasy, Science Fiction, Detective, Romance, Mystery, and Humor.

As all these genres of writing are as different as they sound, the readers, principles, emotions, thinking and basic idea behind all these types of writings are different to each other as well.

Below we define some golden principles for each category.

10.1. Fiction

Fiction is shaped by creativity & imagination of its writer. He's the one who makes up different characters and plot them according to his own storyline and setting. Principles to write for this category are:

- For a good writer, the first principle is to develop his own writing style as the most significant thing about fictional writing is it is totally owned by its writer.
- Theme, Storyline, Characters, Dialogues are of great importance.
- Write dialogues in a natural way to connect with readers. Use Creative ideas to keep the reader connected to your story.

10.2. Non- fiction

Non- Fiction is about real events in the past, as in histsorical writing, or the present. In this genre, no imaginary characters or scenarios are represented. Principles to write for this category are:

- Understand that non- fiction writing is based on facts or conclusions derived from facts and nothing else. But you can always turn your facts into a persuasive story.
- Use emotional language to grab the attention of your reader.
- Be descriptive about characters or scenes and don't go stating the facts in one go, rather play forward and rewind with scenes to keep the suspense alive.

10.3. Novel

A sub category of fiction, the Novel is a book length story plotted with imaginary characters and scenarios. All principles of fictional writing apply to this category and some specific rules for novel writing are:

- ☐ Add variety to your style of writing (characters, moods, and scenes). The Novel is a mixture of emotions and feelings expressed through a theme idea and storyline.
- ☐ Use strong, concrete sentence structure.
- ☐ Avoid using passive voice and unnecessary words, rather write with an optimistic approach sending out positive vibes.

10.4. Short story

Another sub category of fiction, the Short Story is shorter in length than a novel. It usually emphases on one central plot, one main character (with a few added minor characters). Principles for short story writing are:

- ☐ A short story should only be focused on one theme.
- ☐ The story is narrated from the point of view of the central character.
- ☐ A short story always has a climax to end the conflict shown in storyline.

10.5. Drama

Drama is planned to depict life or character involving conflicts and sentiments through action and dialogue usually written for theatre and stage performance. Principles to be followed while writing a drama are:

- ☐ Important things to be considered while writing drama are: Conflict, Characters, Emotions, Story, and Screenplay.

- [ ] It is about orders of events in your plot.
- [ ] Goal is about what your character wants to achieve.

10.6. Fantasy

Another sub category of fiction is Fantasy, a genre of writing in which the plot could not happen in real life e.g. magic, witchcraft or about undiscovered dimensions of the world. Few principles of fantasy fiction writing is:

- [ ] To set this genre apart from other story types is element of imagination beyond any boundaries.
- [ ] While fantasy writing, your story takes place in a completely new world, In order to immerse readers in your world, you must develop your setting thoroughly and thoughtfully.
- [ ] Key to every good story is conflict as the fantasy story usually stretches across multiple books in a series.

10.7. Science Fiction

A type of fiction writing which involves scientific knowledge and technologies for its plot. Important Principle to be considered while writing science fiction is:

- [ ] Writings in this category involve partially true partially fictitious laws or theories of science. It should not be completely unbelievable because then it jumps into the fantasy category.

10.8. Detective

A sub category of fiction is Detective fiction, a genre of writing where a detective works to solve a mystery/crime. Principles of writing a detective novel/story are:

□ The reader must have equal chance with the detective for cracking the mystery. All clues must be plainly specified and described.
□ The offender must be determined by logical conclusions, not by accident or coincidence.
□ Detective fiction should contain no long descriptive passages such matters have no important place in a record of crime and conclusion.

10.9. Romance

Romance writing in old times involved a shadowy, daring, or spiritual story line where the focus is on bravery and strong values, not a love interest. However, today new definition of romance also includes stories that have a relationship issue or love story as central plot. Its Principles are:
□ Ending should be on a happy note.
□ Include a love conflict and revolve all other minor plots around the central theme.
□ Create various adventures or excitement while keeping the spiritual element of love alive in the story.

10.10. Mystery

It is a type in literature that emphases on somebody solving a mystery or a crime. It is correlated to detective fiction. Principles of writing mystery fiction are:
□ For mystery writing it's important to answer these three basic questions: 'What happened? How did it happen? Who did it?'
□ There are different categories in mystery fiction (Hard Boiled, Cozy, Police procedural, Locked room, thriller) all have a different taste of its own.

- ☐ An element of expectation that situation will work out should be kept alive till the very end.

10.11. Humor

Humor is more of a state of art than just a genre for writing. It is an art to make people laugh through a piece of writing. Although some people are naturally funnier than others. Principles for humorous writing are:

- ☐ The content must be appropriate to the interests of the audience, and it must relate well to the personality of the performer.
- ☐ Author needs to learn comedic brainstorming techniques using relations and entertainment guide.
- ☐ Write what amuses you. If you can't be funny, be fascinating. You haven't lost the reader keep them connected.

<u>Conclusion</u>

You are a writer whose ultimate goal is to keep the readers happy and increase your readership as well. The book describes all the topics which a rising writer should be aware of to enhance his/her writing skills. The recipe to become a good writer is very simple yet it requires a lot of practice and determination to be one. Make it your routine to write daily, even if you are writing a single paragraph which followed the basic rules of writing good. You have done a really good job. Besides writing daily, make it your habit to read daily as well. You have no idea how much these two simple habits are going to add to your writing skill. If you can join some writer's community, don't hesitate joining and showing your work there. You can get valuable suggestions from your fellow writers which can add to your knowledge too.

Polish your researching skills. It might seem like a boring task initially, but to publish a content, you must have sound knowledge about it. This will also help you to get your facts correct about any underwork niche. Don't be afraid of writing and rewriting. You are a rising talent in the world of writers, and your consistency and determination is what will keep you going.

Always remember, the saying *practice makes a man perfect* is a truism. If you make this your motto, especially in times when you are not getting any achievement, you will get through successfully.

Write well series

The series that grows with your writing skills. We hope that with us you are getting a little further in achieving literary Olympus.

1. How To Write Your First Book: If You Want to Write - Learn How to Do It. Novel, Short Story, Fiction or Nonfiction Doesn't Matter. Everybody Writes And So Can You!
by Gillian Carson
2. How To Write Better: Take Your Writing To The Next Level Creating Texts That Readers Want To Read
by Gillian Carson